MAXIMIZING DENIM PROFITS

"EFFICIENCY, SUSTAINABILITY, COLLABORATION"

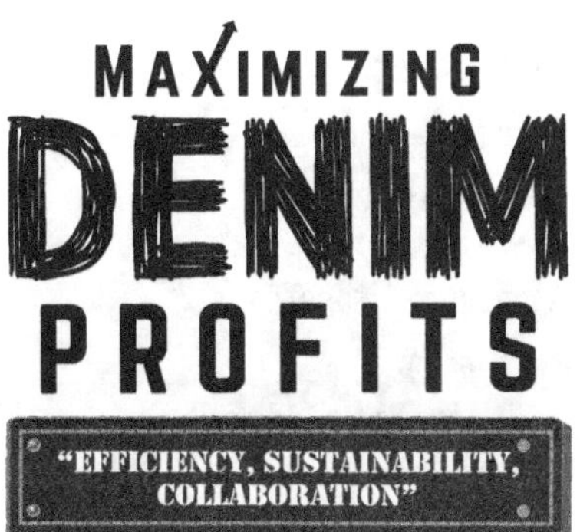

Pankaj Sharma

Worldwide Published by
Pendown Press

PENDOWN PRESS LLP

An ISO 9001 & ISO 14001 Certified Co.,

Regd. Office: 3767A, Kanhaiya Nagar,

Tri Nagar, Delhi-110035

Ph.: 8130886000, 9650072927, 8595249536

E-mail: info@pendownpress.com

Branch Office: 1A/2A, 20, Hari Sadan, Ansari Road,

Daryaganj, New Delhi-110002

Ph.: 011-45794768

Website: PendownPress.com

Edition: 2024

ISBN: 978-93-5554-901-3

Layout and Cover Designed by Pendown Graphics Team
Printed and Bound in India by Thomson Press India Ltd.

Dedication

This book is dedicated to my late father.

In tribute to your ever-helpful spirit and your inspiration to share knowledge with all. Though you may not be here to hold this book in your hands, your presence resonates within its very essence. Your unwavering faith in me continues to light my path every single day.

CONTENTS

❖   ❖   ❖   ❖

Acknowledgments

Δ   *To my dear mother*

Thank you for being my rock, my confidante, and my guiding star. Your unwavering support and sacrifices have fueled my aspirations and nourished my spirit. This book stands as a testament to your unwavering faith in me.

Δ   *To my beloved wife*

This book belongs to you as much as it does to me. It carries the essence of our shared dreams and aspirations. Thank you for standing by my side, for believing in me, and for being the heartbeat of my existence.

Δ   *To my two loving sons*

Your desire to see me achieve something special in life has been my driving force. This book acknowledges my two stars, for you are my constant motivation and source of joy.

Δ   *To my industry seniors*

I've had the privilege of working with the best organizations in our industry. Your guidance and support have helped me bring out the best in myself. I am grateful for your inspiration and encouragement.

With heartfelt gratitude,

Pankaj Sharma

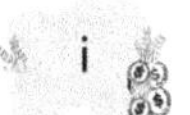

About the Book

Title: Maximising Denim Profits – Efficiency, Collaboration, Sustainability

Δ Introduction:

Welcome to "**Maximising Denim Profits**," a comprehensive guide tailored specifically for CEOs and owners of denim manufacturing units with in-house wash plants. In this book, you'll find invaluable insights and strategies to elevate your denim manufacturing operation to the forefront of the industry. From reducing rejections to fostering a culture of accountability and efficiency, "Maximising Denim Profits" is your roadmap to becoming the premier denim manufacturer in the market.

What to Expect:

1. **Achieve No.1 Denim Manufacturer Status:** Discover proven strategies and best practices to take your denim manufacturing unit to the top spot in the industry. Learn how to differentiate your brand, optimize production processes, and exceed customer expectations to solidify your position as a leader in the denim market.

2. **Reduce Overall Rejections to 2%:** Implement actionable tactics and SOPs (Standard Operating Procedures) to drastically reduce rejection rates in your denim manufacturing operation. From pre-production activities to post-wash quality control measures, this book provides practical solutions to minimize rejections and maximize profitability.

3. **Cultivate a High-Performing Team:** Transform your workforce into a cohesive, accountable, and customer-centric team with the guidance of "Maximising Denim Profits." Explore strategies for talent development, performance measurement, and fostering a customer-focused mindset among your employees. By empowering your team members, you'll create a culture of excellence that drives success in every aspect of your denim manufacturing operation.

Δ Conclusion:

"Maximising Denim Profits" is more than just a book—it's a blueprint for success in the competitive world of denim manufacturing. By leveraging the insights and strategies outlined in this guide, you'll unlock the full potential of your denim manufacturing unit, achieve unparalleled excellence, and secure your position as a leader in the global denim market.

Testimonial

Pankaj Sharma stands out as one renowned professional who has transformed denim processing with a very unique and innovative approach in the textile industry. His knowledge and experimental flair have enabled much product and process innovation, resulting in sustainable growth, resource efficiency, and environmentally friendly production. He is the epitome of promoting sustainable practices in the denim industry with his customer-centric approach and ethical manner. I have had the privilege to work with him on various aspects of product innovation, process automation, and sustainable practices, which position him as a thought leader in the denim processing industry.

Dr. Naresh Tyagi

Chief Sustainability Officer,

Aditya Birla Fashion & Retail Ltd

Testimonial

I cannot recommend the services of Pankaj Sharma as a denim wash expert highly enough. His operational excellence, combined with a genuine commitment to ensuring customer satisfaction, sets a standard that others in the industry should aspire to reach. If you're seeking not just a denim wash but an operational excellence that exceeds expectations, look no further.

Mr. B.M Calla

CEO, Ramdhan Laundries

❖ ❖ ❖ ❖

Testimonial

I whole heartedly endorse Pankaj Sharma for his exceptional contributions to our denim wash operation. His dedication, expertise, and innovative spirit have resulted in substantial improvements, positioning our denim production at the forefront of industry standards. On my behalf, I commend the work he did with Shahi when he was part of the denim team at an early stage.

Mr. Raghavan Ramanujam

CEO and Director, Shahi Exports

Testimonial

I just wanted to share a few thoughts of our journey together at Aquarelle India. Your contribution in positioning Aquarelle India as a 'Denim Tops Specialist' was immense. Your denim know-how has helped us to position for denim tops' business with all our key customers in a much stronger way since you joined Aquarelle India. Working with Pankaj Sharma has been a game-changer for our denim business. Your careful approach and systems that you created to manage and grow this business have helped Aquarelle India to build a strong denim story and business around it. Wishing you good luck in your new endeavor.

Mr. B.M.K. Nagesh

CEO, Aquarelle India Pvt. Ltd

My Journey

My journey in the textile industry has been a fulfilling odyssey, shaped by various experiences and a strong commitment to learning and growth.

As a Textile Chemistry graduate from DKTE Textile Institute, Ichalkaranji, I've enjoyed a 25-year career spanning different aspects of the textile sector. From working in mills to engaging in chemical sales, collaborating with renowned brands to contributing to garment manufacturing units, my professional trajectory has been marked by versatility and a thirst for knowledge.

Throughout my tenure, I've had the privilege of working both in India and abroad, gaining invaluable insights and honing my expertise. A significant highlight of my career has been my involvement in the commissioning and installation of five wash plants, with three of them being denim wash plants. These experiences have earned me a reputation as a denim wash expert, with colleagues jokingly saying denim runs in my veins.

Growing up in a middle-class family, I was raised with the values of generosity and compassion. My parents' unwavering belief in the principle of giving back to society left an indelible mark on me. Their selfless acts of kindness, from helping villagers in securing employment to opening our doors to those in need, instilled in me a deep-seated desire to share my knowledge and experiences with others.

Despite facing challenges, including a two-year setback in pursuing my engineering dreams after high school, I remained determined to succeed. Inspired by my father's aspirations, I eventually found my calling in the textile industry—a path that felt like destiny, given my early exposure to textiles through my maternal grandfather's textile shop.

Driven by a passion for textiles and a hunger for knowledge, I embraced every opportunity to learn and grow. My stint at Resil Chemicals introduced me to the world of garment washing—a revelation that sparked my interest and motivated me to delve deeper into this field. Recognizing a lack of technical expertise in this area, I took the initiative to innovate and improve processes, using my technical skills to make meaningful contributions.

My mantra in life has always been to seek knowledge relentlessly and share it generously. This approach has not only facilitated my professional growth but has also helped me build lasting relationships with industry leaders and peers.

Now, as I embark on the next chapter of my journey as an author, my goal is clear: to pay it forward by sharing the wealth of knowledge and insights I've gained over the years. Through this book, I aim to empower my colleagues in the denim garment manufacturing community, providing them with practical guidance and strategies to enhance their performance and drive organizational success.

In essence, my purpose is twofold to uplift and inspire my fellow industry professionals and to foster positive change and growth within the denim garment manufacturing sector, both in India and beyond. Together, let us embark on this journey of discovery, learning, and transformation.

Introduction

Inclusivity plays a crucial role in addressing the challenges faced by denim manufacturers, particularly in the realm of denim washing. After decades of experience in the industry and overseeing numerous denim wash plants, I firmly believe that inclusivity holds the key to solving many of the common issues.

When we look at the laundry list of problems affecting denim manufacturers—ranging from high rejection rates in washing to delays in deliveries, customer dissatisfaction, shipment delays, and excessive rewashes—it becomes evident that a holistic approach is necessary. Denim, unlike other products, undergoes a significant transformation during the washing process, necessitating the involvement and collaboration of various departments across the entire value chain.

Allow me to elaborate further. In the case of non-denim products, the supply chain can often operate with relative independence. Fabric may be sourced from one location, cut and stitched elsewhere, and then washed and finished at a different site without encountering substantial challenges. This process works because the fabric's appearance and color remain consistent throughout, with only the shape being altered. However, denim presents a unique set of challenges due to its transformational nature post-wash.

For denim, achieving consistency and desired outcomes requires meticulous adherence to standardized operating procedures (SOPs) and seamless coordination among all stakeholders. While SOPs may exist within organizations and seem to be followed, the root of the problem often lies in their fragmented implementation.

Departments operate separately, with communication gaps between marketing and the wash team, fabric teams remaining disconnected from production and marketing, and factories operating independently of the broader strategic objectives. Even with SOPs, the lack of collaboration hampers the achievement of desired results.

The solution lies in creating a culture of inclusivity and collaboration across departments. By breaking down silos and encouraging open communication and cooperation, organizations can address inefficiencies, identify root causes of issues, and implement solutions collectively. This approach not only optimizes operational processes but also enhances overall product quality and customer satisfaction.

In the subsequent chapter, we'll delve deeper into the importance of SOPs and discuss tactics for promoting inclusiveness and teamwork across various departments to address the unique hurdles faced in denim manufacturing. Through prioritizing inclusivity, companies can tap into fresh avenues for productivity, creativity, and success within the dynamic denim industry.

❖　　❖　　❖　　❖

Framework 1

PPC - Practicality, Pre-Production, Communication

The PPC framework, focusing on Practicality, Pre-production, and Communication, serves as a comprehensive approach to address challenges and enhance efficiency in denim manufacturing.

Δ Practicality Process

Making sure denim samples are feasible for bulk production is crucial. This involves a collaborative effort among stakeholders to assess whether the proposed style aligns with infrastructure and capacities. If not feasible, suggestions for necessary alterations should be communicated to the brand promptly. Conversely, if deemed feasible, a thorough discussion on seamless integration into production lines should take place, with all call-outs duly noted and documented.

Δ Pre-production Activity

Pre-production activities are pivotal in streamlining operations. While we usually focus on sewing-related matters, we can improve efficiency by including warehouse tasks like checking fabric quality, shrinkage, and mill packing lists.

Δ Communication

Effective communication is key for successful denim manufacturing. With numerous steps involved from development to shipping, it's imperative that SOPs are not only understood but also well-communicated across all departments. Establishing clear channels of communication ensures transparency and minimizes the risk of mistakes. Visual representations mapping out the communication flow among stakeholders can further enhance comprehension and collaboration.

Δ Case Study

Sharing a case study highlighting the consequences of poor communication emphasizes its importance.

Singh Denim Co. secured a lucrative contract with a prominent fashion brand to produce a new line of premium denim jeans featuring intricate wash effects. Despite having state-of-the-art facilities and skilled personnel, the project encountered significant setbacks due to communication breakdowns at various stages of production.

Δ Consequences of Poor Communication

➢ Misaligned Expectations

- The client provided vague specifications regarding the desired wash effects, assuming Singh Denim Co. understood their preferences implicitly. However, without clear communication channels established, the company's interpretation of the client's vision differed significantly from their expectations.

- As a result, the initial prototypes failed to meet the client's standards, leading to frustration and delays in the production timeline.

➢ Quality Control Issues

- Poor communication between the design and production teams resulted in inconsistencies in wash effects across different batches of denim fabric.

- Without clear guidelines and feedback mechanisms in place, deviations from the desired quality standards went unnoticed until the final inspection stage, leading to costly rework and compromised product quality.

➢ Supply Chain Disruptions

- Inadequate communication with suppliers regarding raw material requirements and production schedules led to delays in sourcing essential components, such as chemicals and dyes.

- These supply chain disruptions further exacerbated production delays and strained relationships with both suppliers and clients.

➢ **Client Dissatisfaction**

- The accumulation of communication errors throughout the production process culminated in dissatisfaction from the client, who perceived Singh Denim Co. as unreliable and unprofessional.

- Despite the company's technical capabilities, the inability to effectively communicate and manage client expectations jeopardized the long-term partnership and future business opportunities.

Δ The Importance of Effective Communication

➢ Clarity and Alignment

Clear communication ensures that all stakeholders are aligned with project objectives, specifications, and timelines, minimizing the risk of misunderstandings and discrepancies..

➢ Efficiency and Productivity

Open channels of communication facilitate seamless coordination among team members, enabling efficient workflow and timely resolution of issues or challenges that may arise during production.

> Quality Assurance

Effective communication fosters transparency and accountability, enabling proactive identification and resolution of quality control issues before they escalate, thereby upholding product quality and customer satisfaction.

> Relationship Building

Strong communication fosters trust and collaboration among clients, suppliers, and internal teams, laying the foundation for long-term partnerships and business success.

Δ Conclusion

The case study of Singh Denim Co. highlights the detrimental consequences of poor communication in denim manufacturing, ranging from misaligned expectations and quality control issues to supply chain disruptions and client dissatisfaction. By emphasizing the importance of effective communication and implementing robust communication strategies, denim manufacturers can mitigate risks, enhance operational efficiency, and build lasting relationships with clients and stakeholders, ultimately driving success in a competitive industry landscape.

When information doesn't reach everyone on time, it can lead to delays, rejections, and damage to our reputation. By emphasizing the detrimental effects of poor communication, the case study underscores the necessity of proactive and transparent communication practices throughout the manufacturing process.

△ *How to Communicate and What to Communicate:*

Communicating effectively involves not only the timely dissemination of information but also the clarity and relevance of the message. By prioritizing transparency and proactivity, factories can avoid potential pitfalls and mitigate risks. The story exemplifies the impact of poor communication, emphasizing the need for robust communication systems and a culture of accountability.

In conclusion, the PPC framework underscores the pivotal role of Practicality, Pre-production, and Communication in mitigating challenges and optimizing efficiency in denim manufacturing. By fostering collaboration, transparency, and proactive communication practices, factories can enhance operational effectiveness and uphold their credibility in the competitive global market.

Framework
2

AMS - Accountability, Measure, Self-Reporting

The AMS framework, focusing on Accountability, Measure, and Self-Reporting, provides a structured approach to enhancing performance and fostering a culture of responsibility within denim manufacturing teams.

> **Accountability:** Accountability is the cornerstone of effective teamwork and organizational success. It means clearly defining roles and responsibilities for each team member, ensuring they understand their contribution to the overall objectives. Management plays a pivotal role in setting these expectations and providing the necessary support and guidance to enable team members to fulfill their duties effectively.

> **Measure:** Measurement is essential for improvement. By collecting data at various stages of the manufacturing process—such as sampling, cutting, stitching, fabric handling, washing, and finishing—management gains insights into performance metrics and identifies areas for enhancement. Analyzing this data allows for the identification of low-hanging fruit opportunities for improvement, guiding targeted interventions to optimize processes and outcomes.

➤ **Self-Reporting System:** Embracing a self-reporting system empowers team members to take ownership of their performance and growth. Rather than relying solely on external oversight and policing, this approach encourages individuals to reflect on their work, identify areas for improvement, and proactively report progress to management. By fostering a culture of openness and self-assessment, self-reporting systems promote accountability, engagement, and continuous improvement within the workforce.

In conclusion, the AMS framework emphasizes the importance of Accountability, Measure, and Self-Reporting in driving performance and fostering a culture of responsibility and continuous improvement within denim manufacturing teams. By clarifying expectations, leveraging data-driven insights, and empowering individuals to take ownership of their development, organizations can enhance efficiency, effectiveness, and overall success in the competitive denim industry landscape.

Δ SOP of full process

PROCESS FLOW CHART FROM DEVELOPMENT TO OCR

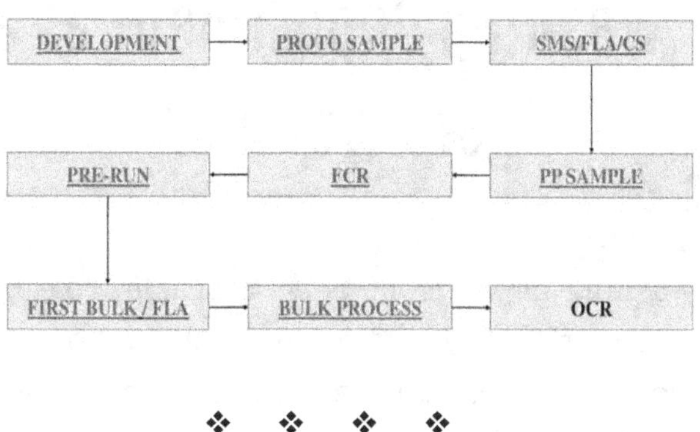

❖   ❖   ❖   ❖

Washing Department as a Stakeholder

The washing department plays a crucial role in denim manufacturing, and effective coordination with all stakeholders is essential to ensure smooth operations and high-quality output. Here are some suggestions on how the washing team can work collaboratively with other departments:

- ➢ Development
  - The washing department should assess if the fabric and wash process are compatible during the development stage.
  - They should also consider garment construction to anticipate any potential issues that may arise during bulk production.
  - All concerns should be addressed during practicality meetings, and relevant information should be communicated to the brand.
- ➢ Fabric
  - The washing team should establish standard operating procedures (SOPs) with fabric mills through their fabric departments.

- Discussions regarding special requirements should occur when receiving head ends or blankets from the mill.

➢ **Stitching**

- Collaboration between the washing and stitching departments is crucial to address any special requirements before production begins.

- Details such as pocket stitching, loop attachment, bartacks, and zipper closure should be discussed during pre-production meetings (PPMs) for each style and order.

➢ **Finishing**

- The washing team should maintain daily communication with the finishing department to share production plans and ensure efficient line planning.

- Finishing should be aware of the realities of the washing process to optimize their operations.

➢ **Marketing**

- Marketing teams should be informed about the status of orders and stay in touch with the washing team for technical details.

- Technical discussions can be streamlined through joint meetings with all stakeholders and the brand.

➢ **PPC (Production, Planning and Control)**

- The PPC team serves as a central point for planning and coordinating activities across departments.

- They should be kept updated on all production-related information and any delays that may affect deliveries.

By fostering effective communication and collaboration among these stakeholders, the washing department can streamline operations, mitigate risks, and ensure the timely delivery of high-quality denim products.

Washing Department as a 'Sutradhaar'

The concept of the washing department serving as the "Sutradhaar" or central figure in denim manufacturing is indeed apt. Here's why the washing department plays such a pivotal role and how it can effectively fulfill this role:

> Central Coordination

- The washing department acts as a central coordinator, linking various departments together.

- By taking charge of setting up systems with the support of top management, the washing head ensures smooth communication and collaboration among all departments.

> Preventive Measures

- By proactively monitoring all stages of production, the washing department can anticipate potential issues and take preventive measures.

- This proactive approach helps avoid last-minute crisis and allows the team to focus on important tasks and innovations that can drive the organization forward.

➢ **Reality Check**

- The washing department provides a reality check by communicating openly and transparently about the challenges and constraints faced during production.

- This transparency fosters better understanding and cooperation among departments, leading to more effective problem-solving and improved overall performance.

➢ **Unique Expertise**

- With their expertise in garment washing, the washing team is uniquely positioned to assess whether the fabric and wash processes are compatible.

- They can predict potential issues that may arise during production and provide valuable insights to other departments.

➢ **Value Addition**

- The washing department adds value to the garment after stitching, making them crucial to the final product's quality and appearance.

- By recognizing their importance and empowering them to lead coordination efforts, organizations can enhance their reputation with brands and customers.

In conclusion, positioning the washing department as the "Sutradhaar" in denim manufacturing acknowledges its central role in coordinating various departments, preventing issues, providing a reality check, leveraging unique expertise, and adding value to the final product. By embracing this role and fostering effective communication and collaboration, organizations can achieve greater efficiency, quality, and success in the competitive denim market.

Δ The Importance of Continuous Flow in Denim Manufacturing

In denim manufacturing, achieving a seamless production flow is essential for meeting deadlines and maintaining efficiency. However, it's often observed that operations come to a halt at the washing department, leading to delays and disruptions throughout the production process. Let's delve into some common reasons behind these interruptions:

- ➢ Shade Discrepancies: Confusion and discrepancies arise when multiple shades are labeled under the same category, affecting the final product's consistency.

- ➢ Shade Matching: If the shades produced during washing don't match the established standards, it can lead to delays as adjustments are needed.

- ➢ Post-Washing Damages: Sometimes, damages are only discovered after the first bulk lot is washed, necessitating rework and halting production.

- ➢ Incomplete Wash Preparation: When washing preparation isn't adequately discussed or executed, it leads to delays as additional support is required from other departments, such as sewing.

To uphold the mantra of "No Stop Once You Say Go," it's imperative to address these issues before they escalate. My philosophy, developed over years of experience, emphasizes resolving conflicts and challenges before fabric cutting begins. This approach ensures that once production starts, it proceeds smoothly until the final product is packed.

Pre-production activities play a crucial role in achieving this seamless flow. Therefore, it's essential for senior team members from each department to be actively involved in pre-production tasks. Unfortunately, it's often the case that these responsibilities are delegated to junior staff, while senior personnel focus on firefighting in production. However, involving experienced team members upfront can prevent the need for firefighting altogether, proving to be more productive in the long run.

In summary, continuous flow in denim manufacturing relies on proactive problem-solving and collaboration among departments. By addressing issues before production commences and involving senior team members in pre-production activities, organizations can minimize disruptions and ensure a smooth production process from start to finish.

Δ Story to explain

Once upon a time, in the bustling denim manufacturing town of Indigo Valley, there stood a renowned denim factory known for its excellent craftsmanship and timely deliveries. At the heart of this factory was the washing department, led by the wise and experienced Washmaster, Mr. Indigo.

One sunny morning, as the factory gears began to turn, a new denim style called "Azure Dream" arrived on the production floor. Excitement buzzed through the air as designers, marketers, and technicians gathered around to examine the fabric samples and discuss the wash process. However, amidst the enthusiasm, Mr. Indigo noticed a potential issue. The fabric's shade variations were subtle but noticeable enough to raise concern. Rather than ignoring it, Mr. Indigo called for an emergency meeting with heads from every department involved in the production of "Azure Dream."

In the meeting, Mr. Indigo emphasized the importance of addressing the shade discrepancies before cutting the fabric. He stressed the need for seamless coordination between departments to ensure a smooth production flow. Together, they brainstormed solutions and established a clear plan of action.

With the issues identified and solutions in place, the fabric cutting began. As the denim pieces made their way through the stitching lines, Mr. Indigo and his team closely monitored the progress, ensuring that every stitch aligned with the predetermined wash requirements.

Days passed, and soon, the first batch of "Azure Dream" denim reached the washing department. With meticulous care, Mr. Indigo and his team began the wash process, following the predefined SOPs and keeping a watchful eye on every detail.

As the denim emerged from the wash cycle, it was evident that the coordinated efforts had paid off. The shades were consistent, the quality was impeccable, and there were no surprises after washing. The denim flowed seamlessly through the finishing lines, ready to be packaged and shipped to awaiting customers.

The success of "Azure Dream" served as a testament to the power of proactive problem-solving and collaboration in denim manufacturing. By addressing potential issues upfront and involving experienced team members in pre-production activities, the factory had achieved its goal of seamless production.

From that day forward, Mr. Indigo and his team continued to lead the charge, ensuring that no obstacles stood in the way of Indigo Valley's reputation for excellence in denim manufacturing. And as the factory gates closed each evening, the echoes of their success reverberated through the valley, inspiring all who crossed their path.

Satisfy Internal Customer to Get Best Award from External Customer

To illustrate the importance of satisfying internal customers to achieve success with external customers, let's delve into a story

In the busy denim factory of Indigo Dreams, there was a sense of excitement as the team got ready to handle a big order from a famous global brand. With deadlines coming up fast and everyone expecting top-notch work, it was clear that seamless collaboration and teamwork were important.

At the helm of the operation was Mr. Denim, the experienced factory manager known for his ability to build a culture of excellence and teamwork. He understood that to deliver exceptional products to external customers, they first needed to satisfy their internal customers – the various departments within the factory.

As the production lines hummed with activity, Mr. Denim gathered his team for a crucial meeting. He emphasized the importance of understanding and fulfilling the needs of their internal customers to ensure smooth operations and timely deliveries.

"Remember, our ultimate goal is to satisfy our external customers, but we cannot achieve that without first satisfying each other," Mr. Denim said firmly." Marketing relies on us to produce high-quality denim, while finishing depends on washing to prepare the garments for their final touches. It's a chain of dependencies, and each link must be strong."

With Mr. Denim's guidance, the team started paying more attention to their colleagues within the factory. The marketing department communicated their requirements clearly to the factory, ensuring that production plans aligned with market demands. In turn, the factory worked closely with the fabric department to procure the finest materials, meeting the specifications outlined by marketing.

Meanwhile, the washing and finishing departments worked closely together to ensure that each garment got the perfect wash and finish, making it more appealing to the final customer. And throughout the process, the PPC team monitored progress, adjusting schedules and resources as needed to keep the production flowing smoothly.

As the weeks went by, Indigo Dreams' commitment to satisfying their internal customers yielded remarkable results. The production lines ran like a well-oiled machine, with hardly any delays and maximum efficiency. And when the time came to deliver the finished denim to the external customer, they did so with pride, knowing that they had met and exceeded expectations at every step of the process.

In the end, the external customer was delighted with the quality and timeliness of their order, showering Indigo Dreams with praise and repeat business. And as Mr. Denim looked out over his factory, he knew that the key to their success lay not just in satisfying external customers but in nurturing a culture of collaboration and excellence among their internal customers.

❖   ❖   ❖   ❖

Create a Data Bank

To effectively address common issues and improve processes in denim manufacturing, creating a comprehensive data bank is essential. Here's how it can be structured:

➢ **Issue Identification:** Begin by identifying the common issues or mistakes that occur regularly in the denim manufacturing process. These could include problems related to fabric treatment, washing techniques, dyeing processes, or finishing methods. Ensure that all stakeholders, including fabric and washing teams, share their experiences to create a full list.

➢ **Data Collection:** Establish a systematic approach to collecting relevant data for each identified issue. This may involve recording information such as fabric specifications, washing parameters, chemical treatments, machine settings, and quality control measurements. Use digital tools and software systems to streamline data collection and storage processes.

➢ **Data Analysis:** Once the data is gathered, perform thorough analysis to identify patterns, trends, and correlations related to the recurring issues. Use statistical techniques and data visualization tools to gain insights into the root causes of these problems. Engage cross-functional teams, including fabric specialists, washing experts, quality control personnel, and production managers, in the analysis process to ensure diverse perspectives are considered.

➢ **Solution Generation:** Based on the findings from data analysis, collaborate with relevant stakeholders to develop effective solutions for addressing the identified issues. Brainstorm innovative approaches, experiment with alternative techniques, and leverage best practices from past experiences to come up with practical solutions. Document these proposed solutions, including step-by-step implementation plans and expected outcomes.

➢ **Documentation and Circulation:** Document all findings, analyses, and solutions in a centralized data bank dedicated to addressing recurring issues in denim manufacturing. Organize the information in a structured format, making it easily accessible to all relevant team members. Establish protocols for regular review and updates to ensure the data bank remains current and relevant. Circulate the documented solutions to all concerned departments and individuals, emphasizing the importance of implementing the proposed measures to prevent future occurrences of the identified issues.

➤ **Continuous Improvement:** Foster a culture of continuous improvement within the organization by encouraging ongoing data-driven decision-making and problem-solving. Regularly monitor key performance indicators (KPIs) related to the addressed issues, track the effectiveness of implemented solutions, and iterate as necessary to achieve sustained improvements. Encourage feedback from frontline workers and encourage them to contribute their insights to further enhance processes and optimize outcomes.

By establishing a robust data bank and leveraging data-driven insights, denim manufacturing organizations can proactively identify, address, and mitigate recurring issues, leading to enhanced efficiency, productivity, and product quality across the production cycle.

Sustainability

Sustainability is a crucial concern in denim manufacturing, and while large-scale solutions like investing in eco-friendly machinery and chemicals are commendable, there are immediate steps that can be taken to achieve sustainability goals. Let's delve into three key aspects: rewashing, rejection rates, and the number of baths used in the process.

- ➤ **Rewashing:** The percentage of garments that require rewashing is a critical metric. By reducing rewashing, not only do you minimize water and energy consumption, but you also increase production capacity. This efficiency translates directly to cost savings and improved profitability.

- ➤ **Rejection Rates:** High rejection rates not only lead to material wastage but also impact the bottom line. By implementing the strategies outlined in this book, such as improved communication and adherence to SOPs, you can significantly reduce rejection rates. This not only improves the quality of your output but also contributes to a healthier profit margin.

- ➤ **Bath Usage:** The number of baths used in the washing process is another area where sustainability gains can be made. By optimizing processes and investing in advanced machinery that operates at lower water-to-liquor ratios, you can reduce the overall water and chemical usage while maintaining or even enhancing the quality of the finished product.

In summary, sustainability in denim manufacturing can be achieved by focusing on these three key areas. By reducing rewashing, minimizing rejection rates, and optimizing bath usage, you can not only improve the environmental footprint of your operations but also enhance your bottom line and customer satisfaction. And perhaps most importantly, by adopting sustainable practices, you can sleep well at night, knowing that you're making a positive impact on both your business and the planet.

1. In our industry, quality is the biggest parameter for running a successful business. One such story is of my friend Ajay. Ajay and I met at a business event in Delhi and then we became good friends. One day during a phone conversation, he told me that last month his large denim consignment, which was supposed to be shipped abroad, got rejected due to quality issues, causing him significant losses. When I asked him further, he told me that he had to take a loan from the bank to complete the order. Upon hearing this, I asked him why he didn't tell me about it earlier, and I decided to visit his factory the next day to inspect the Quality Parameters created by his team and meet his colleagues. The next day, after about two hours of inspection, I found several loopholes in the washing process which had led to the cancellation of their consignment. After that, I prepared a report and gave them some suggestions.

    Their team carefully implemented those suggestions, and gradually, results started to come in. After a few days, Ajay invited me back to his company. When I arrived there, I found that there had been a significant improvement in their work methods. They were now following every step meticulously, and there was a happy environment among their internal team. Now, whenever I meet Ajay, he talks about this decision, and he's extremely happy with it.

2. Rajesh Arora, a denim manufacturer from Punjab, was facing challenges in bringing sustainability to his business, despite having a decent operation. Their rejection rate had surged to 5%, causing significant concern as excessive rewashing and bath usage led to increased expenses. Although the business was profitable, Rajesh feared that the current trajectory might lead to losses in the near future. One day, their marketing head shared my contact information and advised seeking my expertise. Shortly after, they reached out to me, and we scheduled a meeting. During the meeting, we discussed their concerns, and I suggested various solutions, such as methods to reduce rewashing and how the SOPs I developed could assist them, along with strategies to minimize bath usage. Feeling confident after finding solutions to their concerns, they decided to rework on these methods. Six months later, they saw significant improvements, with their rejection rate now at only 2.5-3%. Their business not only became successful but also reduced expenses drastically, with rejection rates almost negligible.

Conclusion: Two Choices

After delving into the valuable insights provided in this book, you're likely feeling empowered to tackle the challenges that have long plagued your denim manufacturing operation. From the frustrations of high rejection rates to the inefficiencies in communication and coordination among departments, the struggles you've faced are clearly illustrated throughout these pages.

Now, as you stand at a crossroads, you have two distinct paths before you.

The first option is to take charge into your own hands, armed with the knowledge and strategies provided here. With your dedicated team by your side, you can begin implementing the practical frameworks and innovative approaches detailed in these chapters. You'll work tirelessly to streamline your processes, reduce rejections, and foster a culture of accountability and sustainability within your organization.

But perhaps you recognize the complexities of the challenges you face, and you understand that true transformation requires expert guidance and support. In that case, the second option beckons—a partnership with the author of this book, a seasoned veteran with decades of experience in the denim industry.

By reaching out to the author, you open the door to a wealth of specialized knowledge and personalized guidance tailored to your unique needs. Together, we will dissect the specific pain points that have hindered your progress and develop targeted solutions to address them head-on. With the author's expert guidance, you'll navigate the complexities of denim manufacturing with confidence, unlocking new levels of efficiency, profitability, and sustainability along the way.

So, which path will you choose? Will you move ahead independently, armed with the insights you've gained from these pages? Or will you seize the opportunity to collaborate with a trusted expert, accelerating your journey towards a brighter, more prosperous future for your denim manufacturing enterprise? The choice is yours.

Call To Action

Are you ready to revolutionize your denim manufacturing operation and overcome the challenges that have held you back for too long? The time for change is now, and you have two powerful choices at your fingertips:

- ➤ **Take Action Independently:** Equip yourself with the insights and strategies from this book and rally your team to implement transformative initiatives. Dive into the practical frameworks outlined here and embark on a journey of innovation and improvement. Seize the opportunity to lead your organization to new heights of success, one step at a time.

- ➤ **Partner with an Expert:** Recognize the value of expert guidance and support in navigating the complexities of denim manufacturing. Reach out to the author of this book, a seasoned industry veteran, and unlock a wealth of specialized knowledge and personalized assistance. Together, you'll develop targeted solutions tailored to your unique challenges, accelerating your path to sustainable growth and prosperity.

The choice is yours, but remember, the future of your denim manufacturing enterprise depends on the actions you take today. Choose wisely and embark on a journey towards a brighter, more profitable tomorrow.

Call To Action

To explore collaboration opportunities and learn more about how to implement these strategies effectively, contact us at  *[pankajsharma.kiddopanti@gmail.com]*.

Let's transform your denim manufacturing operations together.

❖　❖　❖　❖

www.ingramcontent.com/pod-product-compliance
Lightning Source LLC
LaVergne TN
LVHW020051160726

843469LV00043B/1593